# difficult beauty

# difficult beauty

## Rambles, Rants and Intimate Conversations

### Lauren Crux

Many Names Press
Blue Lake, California

Cover and interior design by Victoria May

Cover photos by Lauren Crux

Author photo by Victor Schiffren


ISBN: 978-1-944497-08-8

Library of Congress Control Number: 2022951315


Lauren Crux, www.laurencrux.com

Kate Hitt, Many Names Press khitt@ManyNamesPress.com
+1-831-728-4302


This edition by Many Names Press is distributed and available worldwide through Ingram and Amazon. Please support the environment and reduce the carbon footprint by buying books at your local independent bookstore, which can be found at Indiebound.org. Special discounts are available for bulk purchase by contacting the publisher or author.

*and still the tiny jiggles of light persist*
*as though some precedent of joy insisted on having its way—*
*a full tank, a sunny day, a mail box stuffed with envelopes.*

    —Kathleen Fraser, *Coincidental*


*I think what you are supposed to do is stay in the midst of life.*

    —Agnes Martin

Dear Reader,

I thought you might like to know that this book did not start out to be a book. Originally it was an epistolary project I began during a particularly challenging time when I didn't have much time. I began to write short pieces I called *little rambles*. The word *ramble* was whimsical and liberating—I could follow my mind wherever it wanted to go. No pressure. I wanted my cow to be happy, so I gave her a large meadow.

Then I decided to pair each ramble with one of my photographs, one that would be in a conversation with the ramble rather than illustrate it. I printed these on small double-sided photo cards, which forced an economy of style, a challenge in itself (I can be wordy). Finally, I mailed them via post to friends, to artists and writers whose lives and work inspired me, or to anyone who asked for one. They were a gift.

At first I thought I would write only ten—but over a five-year period the rambles kept coming. So I kept writing. I aspired to an intimacy with all things—the absurd, the horrific. The beautiful. The recipe for magic mineral vegetable broth. Sometimes I just wanted to reach out and ask if you were there.

I hope this book gives some respite from all the mess. Time for reverie, laughter, a good cry. Solace.

With deep affection,
Lauren

They say the post office is becoming obsolete.
I find this sad. It's not that I'm overly fond of our
funky old downtown post office, with its limited
parking, fluorescent lights, and long lines, but
still I am amazed that I can drop this letter into the
banged-up blue metal collection box on Front Street
and it will find its way. From my hand to your hand.

An email is efficient and perhaps cost-effective,
but it lacks the warmth, the physical materiality
of paper. Something I can touch and hold on to.
Lacks a certain you-ness—the stationery you
choose, the envelope, stamp, your signature.
Of time taken. Of time passing. The Pony Express
was short-lived and never profitable.
But it captured the imagination.

Let's talk soon. It is a melancholy day
but that does not mean it is not beautiful.

*There are flowers that open when they hear birds sing.*

We know that human hearts open when they hear
birds sing—unless of course it is a mockingbird in
the acoustically perfect courtyard of a Berlin apartment
singing its entire repertoire throughout the moon-bright
night until dawn, or the harsh screeching of a blue jay
in the patio at Tassajara Zen Center eyeballing your
sandwich—in which case your heart might be filled
with thoughts of bird murder. But the idea of flowers
opening to birdsong, well that is so damn beautiful
Keats would weep.

And perhaps flowers opening to birdsong is only
partially true and not borne out by science,
but I like to think there is always a place for
true enough.

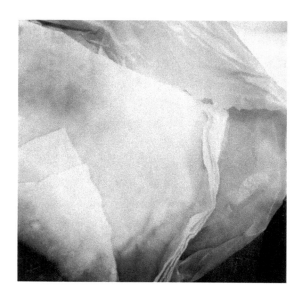

Do you remember life before Google?
I mean, it's all out there now, amazingly so:
how to rescue a bat that's flown into your house,
green drinks for cancer patients, the phone number
of a hotel in Portland.

Stunning really—you can ask anything and someone
before you has asked the same question and someone
else has provided an answer: how to breathe, how to cut
your cat's toenails, how to make a bomb or a peach pie.

Sometimes I prefer to guess, or to try and remember.
Sometimes I enjoy not knowing—the spaciousness of
curiosity itself.

Sometimes I like the tenderness of asking,
*Would you like to be held?*

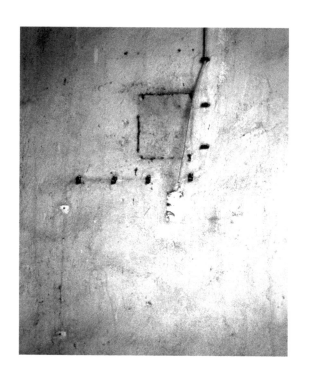

I met a man from the South, an old man, a kind man.
I asked him if he had any children. *Oh yes*, he said,
*four kids*. I asked if they were still at home. *Oh no*,
he said, *they all done went*.

It's one of those weeks:
The car needs a repair.
The computer died.
The microwave's thunking.
The cat needs four teeth pulled.
Pluto is squared with Uranus.
And Scorpio, if you trust the astrologers,
is up to mischief.

I just learned that if you can't smell peanut butter
with your left nostril, it is a sign of early-onset
Alzheimer's. I am off to the store for peanut butter.
If anyone asks you where I am, just tell them,
*She done went*.

Someone asked the Zen master: *How is God defined?*
The answer: *How do you eat the ocean with a fork?*
This left me speechless. Which I guess was the point.

*Have you ever seen a cat not be graceful,* the master
asked. One could argue that a cat throwing up a hairball
is not graceful, but that's nitpicky. The point is, we are
what we are and we could leave it at that and be happy.

Then there's my favorite question from the poet
Pablo Neruda:

> *Where is the center of the sea?*
> *Why do waves never go there?*

I sit down to my lovely bowl of squash apple soup
and once again reach for a fork.

Finally! Rain at 6:50 a.m., Feb. 2, 2014.
Groundhog Day, Santa Cruz, CA. I'm up early,
reading, writing. The boy cat is frapping.

A cat needs to frap (Frenetic Random Activity Periods)
to keep its neurocircuitry working. It is not having fun.
Those of us watching are usually laughing, however.

Frapping is not play: play involves galumphing,
which is fun. This distinction seems important—like
the difference between a bread knife and a tomato
knife. Each has a distinct function even if they look
somewhat alike.

Would that I could when faced with the unbearable,
fling myself into the air, gyrate, and yowl. Streak
about in a crazed frenzy. Then be done with it.
Then take a nap.

A cat has to frap (and nap) to be a cat.
A human has to be kind to be human.

I knew there was no escape, but I figured a little trip
now and then wouldn't hurt. So I went to southern
Spain. There I discovered *sol y sombra*, sun and shade,
unlike anything I had known. No ambiguity, no grays,
no wavering horizons, just intense light and shadow.
I felt unable to describe the harsh beauty—of the
landscape, of the people. The shadows eluded me,
though I felt their presence everywhere.

The women were sensuous and tough. *Fuerza.*
Strength, radiated from the lines and angles of their
faces, their bodies. They made direct eye contact
without flinching. They would not give way on a
narrow street. They liked making me step aside.
At first I thought, fondly, that every woman I saw
was a lesbian.

I lived in Granada for three months, long enough to
stop feeling like a tourist. When the Spanish Civil War
broke out, the first thing the fascists did was kill
all the poets and artists because, *They made people
think.*

Years later, here in the United States, I am still
trying to write about shadows. Shadows and.

8

I'm a Taurus and my motto has long been—*More
is More*. I'd rather read a novel than a short story.
I adore the long slow movie, the long sentence
that travels for two pages (I've just finished reading
Proust). I'll take a backpacking trip over a short walk.
I would rather cook a long meal than get take-out.

But there are times when less really is more:
The single tulip in the vase. A Zen koan. A simple,
*Yes* or *No*. Nothing else necessary or even possible.

Once in my thirties I was hiking in Nepal along a
treacherous narrow trail that was inches from a cliff-
edge that dropped straight down 1500 feet to a
gorgeous archetypal rushing river. My foot slipped
on some stones in the path and I fell—one leg dangled
over the edge, the other buckled below me on the trail.
If I moved at all in the wrong way I would plummet
to my end. There was nothing to grab on to. I worried
that breathing too hard might send me over. Or calling
out for help.

The young woman behind me, a kind and gentle soul
(the rest of the trekking group had gone on; we were
the last two), was still. All she said, quietly, but loud
enough for me to hear and to corroborate that I was
indeed in a shit-load of trouble, was—*Jeez, Lauren*.

This morning early, practicing Qigong in a mountain meadow—*Bringing Down the Heavens, Swimming Dragon, Cloudy Hands…* the sun reaches over the hill and warms my back. No wind. A good thing. (The masters advise that one should not practice Qigong in a thunderstorm or when it is too windy.)

Two deer graze nearby. The locals. They keep their distance. There is also a mountain lion, a flock of wild turkeys, coyotes, bobcats. I feel silly saying this, but they all seem so *natural*—how do I fit in? Final pose: feet together, eyes closed—*Bamboo Swaying in the Wind.*

Later, the deer raise their heads, stand motionless, then spring into the dry brush. A Cooper's hawk swoops but misses its prey. A song sparrow sits on a tuft of grass. I have a friend who laments the way of the world. He carries on. He hopes his beautiful art will mean something. I ask if his words are a rant or a lament. *Both*, he says, *they are both.*

Oh the things we think we will never forget:
that story about the cow; our first childhood
address and phone number; the word for *waste-
basket*. And I never seem to recall the word
*transgressive* when I need it.

In my dreams I remember how to fly. I can ski
with elegance and grace. My Spanish is fluent.
But yesterday when a friend asked me, I could
not remember how old I was. Oddly, it was not
a funny moment, but terror is too strong a word.
I like *perturbation*.

This morning, all is well. Mostly.
There's a serious drought in California.
The *Farmer's Almanac* predicted rain.

I remember rain.
Home was 1669 West 29th St.,
Vancouver, BC., Canada.
Phone: Cherry 8838.

It is 2014.
I'm pretty sure I am sixty-seven.

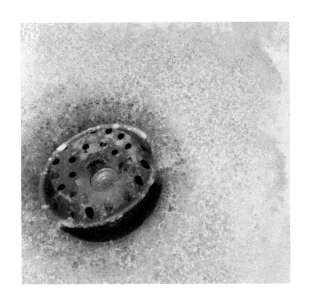

Some Benefits of Being Home with a Stomach Flu

Reading: a book of essays, a mystery, some poetry,
Lao Tzu, and *iPhone 5 for Dummies*.

Naps: the boy cat serenely stretched out along my legs;
the muscular substance of him; the comfort of our
layered descent into *Rest*.

A baked potato: all the white foods I don't usually eat
and don't particularly like, at this moment soothing.

Television: a fictional drama about a woman with
cancer watched with my lover who has cancer.
(The show's fiction helps our reality.)

Time to talk with friends without rushing off to
chase after dragons' eggs.

I re-thread the tie on my hoodie. One of those
annoying little things I've put off. It turns out
to be easy, even pleasing. Oh, I get it:
*Chop wood, carry water.*

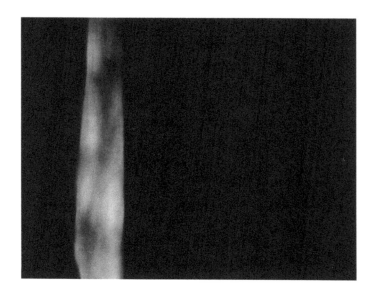

A poet writes: *why and why and why.*
There is no question mark at the end.
She is not really asking a question.
She is evoking an agony.
She trusts we get the drift.

A Buddhist teacher writes:
*A heart at peace asks no questions.*
(What can you say to that?)

*I read the news today, oh boy...*
(They've been playing the Beatles
all week on the local radio station.)

I have so many questions.
*Why and why and why.*

So many shadows—
my constant companions.

## Life Review

My favorite childhood pastime: Riding my make-believe horse over make-believe hills, through make-believe canyons, with my kind, real-life, flesh-and-blood, black and white collie, whose name was Angel.

Odd thing I liked to do: Hammering nails into the branches of our cherry tree, tying string between the nails, pretending I was building something.

I have been listening to an immense silence.
Yes, the meadowlarks and song sparrows sing
their territorial hearts out, the coyotes wake me
early with their maniacal howling, a soaring hawk
screeches. But today is so quiet, I think I can hear
the pillbugs—I love to say their name—*Armadillidiidae*—
scuttling slowly along the walkway.

I ask a composer if this place, the vistas of meadows,
woods, and ocean, is affecting his music. He answers
that he had forgotten silence, that he thought all space
in his head was to be filled with thoughts. *What a pity.*

One afternoon I sit outside his studio. I listen to him
play in honor of Bach's birthday the Sonata in E-flat
Minor. His music now softer, quieter. Spacious.

Bacon. Bacon & eggs & spinach & cheese
on warmed pita bread with salsa. Oatmeal &
strawberries & blueberries with coconut milk.
Tea, green & black. Coffee, espresso & decaf.
Conversation: last night's dream, a poem we read,
our favorite cooking show.

Silent, we sit side by side. We look out at the rainy,
windy, foggy day. *OK, time to go*, one of us says,
then each of us in turn, *Yes, time to go*. No one
moves. The fire in the woodstove warm and
compelling. Ahead of us the blank page, the
empty studio.

Years ago, a drawing instructor told his young
students that for over forty years he had drawn
every day no matter what. One student enthused,
*Oh, how exciting—to draw every day!* The
instructor laughed, *Only a fool faces himself
in the mirror every day.*

I am studying the genetics of calico cats; taking
formal and informal photographs of tissue boxes,
and studying the design and psychology of contemporary
sans serif fonts. Sometimes I write.

Freud thought that people over 50 weren't educable.
Plato thought that 50 was a good time to begin
philosophy. A male art critic declares that the only
creative work you are going to do that matters happens
between the ages of 25 and 50. After that you spend
your time dying. Oh dear, at first I typed *dyking*:
I like that—*Sorry, I can't think right now or write,
dance, paint, bake a princess cake, I'm busy dyking.
After that, I'll be busy dying.*

Today I am doing many of the things I'm not supposed
to be able to do—thinking, writing, researching,
playing, laughing, watching birds, making a video
with friends.

I am so down with the late, great, American writer,
Grace Paley—who, by the way, played a mean game
of table tennis right into her eighties—*It's all life
until death.*

It came to me as I was lying down for a lunch-time nap; I didn't have pen and paper so I grabbed my phone and began to record. It was something I'd been trying to think through for a long time. The first sentence: *How do we know what really matters?* It isn't an original question and I did not have the answer, but I had figured out new ways to understand the dilemma. Words flowed, untroubled and honey-sweet. When I finished, I opened my eyes excited to read, but the screen was blank. Nothing—except for the first sentence—*How do we know what really matters?*

I dreamt last night that Governor Jerry Brown
invited me to a party at the White House. (He and
I were an item: I told his kids I'd be staying over.)
I worried about what to wear—my current wardrobe
clearly inadequate. Should it be a full-length black
dress, or an elegant tux by Armani—the sophisticated
dyke look? I was leaning towards the tux.

All morning, the dream remains oblique. I share it
with friends for fun, but also with the hope that a
thoughtful response might jog in me an understanding.
No such luck, although everyone voted for the tux.

Sometimes we don't get to know what comes next.
But there is relief in letting go. I have a favorite
Zen koan: *I have an agreement with the universe;
it can rain whenever it wants to.*

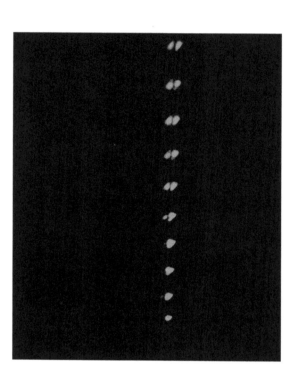

On our weekly walk, a friend tells me she wants
to have more commas in her life. It takes me half a
beat before I understand what she is saying; before
I laugh; before I say, *Good for you*; her life often
like a run-on sentence that leaves the reader breathless
until thirty-six pages later a period brings to a close
a wondrous exuberance.

I've always loved the dash, but lately I am drawn to
semi-colons, which meet a different kind of need;
they offer a longer pause. They also appeal to my
residual Canadianism; a bit more formal, they
step in and bring order to my fractured life while
remaining open to moments before and after.

Sometimes these days, I catch myself not breathing;
as if I could protect myself from life's horrors by not
inhaling; as if a period could save me; or brackets; or
a blank page. This is not what is meant by learning to
be still.

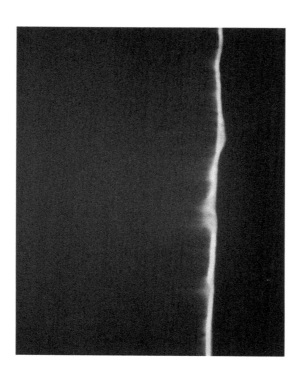

Last night a new friend, a painter from Germany,
said she found that our northern California landscape
stripped her of all that was familiar—a big city, a
bicycle, constant movement, phone calls, emails...

Here, in acres of undeveloped land filled with coyotes
and bobcats and mountain lions and deer and red-tailed
hawks and white-tailed rabbits and purple finches and
blue jays and rattlesnakes and endless pill bugs and a
dog named Hank and a kind man named Tom, she lost
her familiar ways of escape. In all this silence, she fell
back on *herself*. Discovering what she was made of
without all the props. *And this is a good thing*, she
declared. *But I still don't like the snakes.*

I'm OK with the snakes. As a kindness to my friend,
I walk in front so they will strike me first.

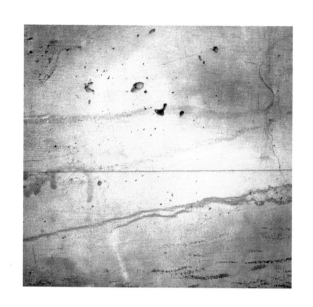

Wislawa Szymborska declared that poems about
spring are disqualified. How about summer?
How about one of those perfect summer days—
hot, but not enough to induce an apathetic torpor—
a slight breeze, tender on the skin; the kind of quiet
that invites you into a deep down inside place?

Meandering down a country road, I had the thought
that I'd like to hear the voices of my ancestors (I had
been reading Joy Harjo's *Crazy Brave*)—something
profound would be nice, although I would settle for
basic guidance—*Which path should I follow now?*

What I did hear—the faint rustle of bay laurels,
the river running slow, my footsteps gentle on the
pavement—was not profound.    I paid attention.

The Buddhist practice of Tonglen (giving and taking) is my favorite: A practice of embracing pain and allowing the heart to transmute anything. *Breathe in suffering; breathe out a wish that we may all be free from suffering.* I think of it as a kind of homeopathy— using poison as medicine.

A friend who is close to retirement is faced with a decision to raise two 11-year-old children whose mother, a relative, is a meth addict and cannot care for them. My friend wants to keep the kids out of the system. She has trouble imagining how her life will change.

My lover is told that radiation will probably kill any cancer cells that remain in her breasts, but the radiation might permanently damage her heart. She is asked *What would you like to do?*

At a retreat, I make a bowl of kale. I sauté it with garlic and olive oil and lemon so it will be ready for my lunch the next day. I add chopped Kalamata olives as a final touch. Then someone else eats it. I feel mad and tighten up with resentment. My lover says to me, *Suffering has many faces.*

I wrote a friend that I had been feeling crabby all
week. She suggested that I actually might be feeling
despondent. I was, after all, following the news: the
beheadings, bombings, wars, more wars, attacks,
retaliations, the daily devastations that one might
sum up in part as the colossus of failed masculinity.

But this week of despair I've been thinking about
what isn't in the news: the more than 200 girls who
were abducted in Nigeria who are still missing and
whom we seem to have forgotten; the women and girls
in Afghanistan that the US was going to liberate and
whom we seem to have forgotten; the women whose
hands and breasts were cut off by soldiers in Rwanda
and the Congo; the ongoing attacks on women in
Bosnia, Syria. Iraq. I've been thinking about the fact
that the mass rape of women is a constant and
intentional tactic of war while save the women
is often a rallying cry for war.

I try to hold everything dear, but at times
it seems beyond me. I feel scraped raw.

Life Review

Where were the places of comfort?

Rocking Horse
Bananas
Flannel sheets
Thumb

Dolls never satisfied

I woke up early and ran out in a bathrobe and sandals
to uncover the water catchment bucket. Then I stood
and took in that distinctive musty-sweet smell of first
rain on warm dry earth—petrichor—a mix of plant oils,
bacterial spores, and ozone. A poetic blend from the
Greek for *stone* and *blood of the gods*.

Two ducks fly away from the ocean, heading upriver.
My lover is writing a memorial speech for her brother,
who took his life months ago. I am avoiding going to
the gym and instead tidying up for the house cleaner.

This rain is only a drop in the bucket as they say.
It does not begin to replenish our drought-depleted
lakes or reservoirs. It is not enough—technically.
But how good it is right now.

A friend writes that she is single for the first time in
twenty-one years; she is coming to town and could we
have lunch. No matter how we may stop in our tracks
from time to time in awe or bewilderment, it all
continues on.

I've just noticed that cats spend an inordinate amount of time grooming. I heard it and now that I've noticed, it's like trying not to think of white polar bears, or having an earworm from a song on the radio. Speaking of which, I heard a bluesy version of *Sitting Here in Limbo* by Chris Webster, which I loved, but now it's stuck on repeat in my brain—*Sitting here in limbo...*

My lover is in Year Two of post-cancer recovery. There is no longer a medical team tracking and directing treatment. It is up to her now. We are both worn out, dislocated. In limbo. She feels awful, though she looks great. There is something to be said about style.

And those cats of mine are grooming again. A moment of play is interrupted to trim a toenail, lick a shoulder. They don't know that next week they will have most of their teeth pulled. Rescue kitties. Gingivitis. Common.

Me? The body deteriorates. I'm waiting to get a new knee, as soon as the weather warms. Even the possibility of being out of pain is sweet. My heart aches for us all.

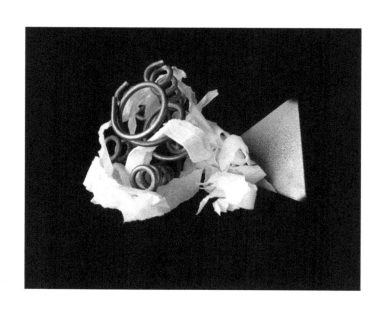

## 25

A therapist friend was talking about her *ancient insecurities*. Actually, what she said was her *anxious insecurities*, but I prefer ancient, impervious to any present-day reality. My evil twin sums up mine by saying I suffer from *Terminal and Incurable Self-Doubt*.

Have you noticed that talking about self-doubt is more acceptable than talking about your evil twin? Something about the word evil gets people agitated, at least in Santa Cruz, the spiritual center of the West. People feel the need to correct or condemn, insisting on the power of the positive. Too bad, I think, because my evil twin often has something valuable to contribute, despite her irreverence, ill-tempered demeanor, and tendency to periodically pick up a rifle and fire it into the ceiling.

No, I'm not going to talk about evil today. Just Ancient Insecurities: Why can't I decide what I want for lunch? Or put in my ten thousand hours and become really good at something? And what about all that inner peace I should have acquired in these golden years of mine? Already I can hear—*Get over it. No mud, no lotus.*

## 26

I was driving home and listening to the news:
The Saudis had just called off a second flogging
of a young man until the wounds from his first flogging
were healed enough to resume more flogging. I pause
here because sometimes the way something is said—
the tone, the sentence structure together with appalling
content—collide into the absurd. The announcer's
dispassionate tone as if reporting the weather...well,
I laughed. For about a second. Then I distracted myself
by wondering how a great comic might take this one on
and skewer it. Remember Richard Pryor? He set himself
accidentally on fire and then turned it into brilliant comedy.
I think I was outsourcing my distress. I have a profound
capacity for distraction.

When I arrived home there was a text from my closest
friend. She was traveling in India with her mother.
One of her fellow travelers had just projectile vomited
on the place of the Buddha's enlightenment. It happened
so fast that all the pilgrims who followed stepped in it.
Always generous of spirit, her conclusion: *The world
is full of shit everywhere you look, and yet light beams
out from so many crannies.*

## 27

I wanted to shoot the rooster. A screechy, scrawny, undignified creature that my neighbor C. adopted and added to his small brood. C. promised he would get rid of the rooster six months ago, then next week, then Sunday, then tomorrow…

Neighbor A. said he'd loan me his rifle. Neighbor D. said he was going to sue. I just wanted to sleep. I wanted not to be lied to.

C. didn't think he was lying. I didn't think he was lying; he was just not telling the truth. I wondered; What is the difference between lying and not telling the truth? Then I stopped caring about the difference between lying and not telling the truth. I wanted the rooster gone.

C. didn't believe me that the rooster started his lunatic shrill at 2 a.m. and continued non-stop until 5 a.m. when he mysteriously fell silent. C. thought I was lying. Or exaggerating.

Ferocity is not my strong suit—polite Canadian etc., but I rallied to the cause: *The rooster goes or you die!* Not exactly what I said, but I was fierce and determined.

The rooster is gone—C. never said how or where. The other neighbors are grateful. I am sleeping again. But C. doesn't talk to me anymore, although we do nod or wave in passing, our shadows briefly touching then sliding apart.

## 28

After falling back asleep this morning, I had a dream that consisted only of fragments. It lacked my usual cohesive narrative style. There was an uncomfortable bed in an impoverished hotel room   I was lying side by side with a friend     a black cat spread-eagled against the window violently biting at the Venetian blinds     outside a woman and her daughter calling to each other     a handyman storing his sponge mop in a refrigerator     a black ocean unfurling between two industrial brick buildings     perfect waves except for nowhere to go and all the crud of industrial waste     a forgotten wallet     a blue sweatshirt in the back seat of a car     then seamlessly in front of me a landscape  a landscape I want to drive into     in black and white wide-open     barren and majestic.

I've had a nasty cold; my ribs hurt from coughing.
Politics are rank. My spirit is congested.
Life seems a mean dark grey.

Oh, but right now, as I write this with my girl cat asleep on my legs, a chickadee gathers the cat's fur from the outdoor cat bed. Softening her spring nest with her predator's fur. The bird, the cat, the human. Perilous, entangled life.

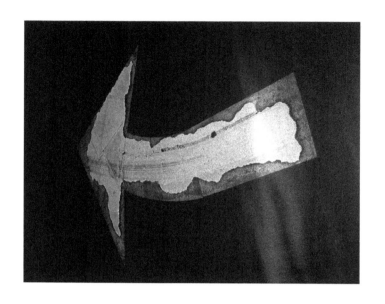

## 29

Yesterday I left with just enough time. But it was not enough time to allow for lane-closures, tree-trimming, and street-sweeping. A side road saved me 10 minutes but I had already lost 30. I called ahead, to say I'd be there but late. I drove at 80 and arrived in 20. I took the wrong exit, got lost, and hit every red-light possible. Then I remembered that I had forgotten to bring what I was supposed to return. Moving on, I left my notes in the car as well as my phone, both of which I needed. When I left to go to the next place, I turned the wrong way, then back around and took a right too soon onto the wrong street. At last I got to where I was going, but I entered the wrong number for the parking space and didn't pay for enough time. I added time but in the wrong way, so I lost time as well as money. When I headed home, early I thought, the traffic was so thick that I stopped at a store to pass the time and let the traffic thin and went to buy white pants. I left with grey pants. I went to another store to ask about my computer but needed my phone, which I had left in the car, again. I made it back in town just in time to buy fresh peaches and corn from the farmer's market before it closed. Then home. Then a breath.
Dinner.

How to end a day entirely spent going the wrong way a little too fast.

## 30

I have a cat who aspires to be a lap cat. She will tentatively put down one paw onto my lap and I can tell *she's thinking about it*, but she doesn't circle and settle. If I read in the morning she likes to lie on my legs with her head facing my feet and her tail stretched out straight behind her. She is content unless I shift, even slightly, in which case she leaps off, tail twitching, to find another resting place, one that involves the solidity of furniture or dirt. One might call her a Very Sensitive Cat, but I resist diagnosis, so instead I'll just call her fussy.

She is an accomplished hunter and, unlike her brother who does not like confrontation, but who is an excellent lap cat, she is the one that protects the property from invading neighbor cats. She is also fearless—or foolhardy, depending upon perspective. We've had to rescue her from tree-tops and other misadventures more than once.

I sometimes wonder which of us will outlive the other. She's nine years older than me in cat years, but she has more lives to spare than I do. On the other hand, as a Zen monk lost in the desert without water said to his companion, *Survival is overrated.*

## 31

Our blue-eyed boy cat, unlike his sister, is the perfect lap cat. He lands, circles, and settles without a fuss. He purrs softly, doesn't drool, and doesn't kneed. I can shift positions, heave him around, and he remains unperturbed, a model of resiliency. However, if you accidentally stumble into him walking in the dark, or close the refrigerator door on his tail, as my lover did when he was a kitten, it will take him weeks to forget or forgive, if ever. His stare is withering. In the face of these transgressions he is not resilient.

He also can be hugely annoying—demanding food, a lap, play, whatever, with his distinctive rasping meow. If he wasn't so stunningly handsome I might be more peevish with him. But I am a sucker for beauty, and this guy— long and lean, tall, muscular, white fur, grey face, tail, and paws, and piercing blue eyes—well, he's the cat's pajamas, as they say.

I'm a therapist by trade and know a lot about trauma— cats, humans, elephants—we can all be hurt. Our hard- wiring changes. We don't all recover, that's the bad news. Many of us heal, that's the good news. Our boy cat's made it most of the way. Me too.

## 32

Well, damn, it's that mortality thing again: It hits me
sometimes like a dragon having pyroclastic night terrors.
I can be hyperbolic at times, but today my aging body,
its slow undoing, feels like a catastrophe.

My new knee is three months old. It's coming along,
but the bionic life is not without difficulties. A little like
dog training, you need lots of patience, persistence, and
love. My wrists are shot and I have a permanently bent
forefinger from a disintegrated joint, which shouldn't,
but does, cause me shame.

Knees, wrists, shoulder, hips—*It's just genetic bad
luck*, my kind surgeon said. But I keep wondering
if I ate too much sugar.

So far the mind still works, but I'm losing nouns.
I've spent so many years in love with verbs, but now
that my nouns are leaving home, I feel an empty-nest
thing going on. I miss them. Right now I am trying
to remember the name of the famous author who,
when asked if she was a feminist, said, *I've been a
woman so long, why wouldn't I want to be on my
own side*. Her name will come to me, eventually,
maybe. In the meantime, I am learning to work the
earth of my heart.

## Life Review

(What were your dreams?)

The first and worst—a nightmare:
A car crash. An eruption of flames.
My mother trapped inside
      screaming.

I am still afraid of fire.

Favorite: I could breathe underwater.
*Le Poisson. Frisson.*
So real, I tried it all the next day.

Serial: Flying
At first I was clumsy, but with practice I soared.
Some nights I cruised low over cities. Once I flew
to Spain. Most often it was wide-open blue that
satisfied. I miss flying. It's been years.

Spinning and spiraling. I was a dolphin in space.

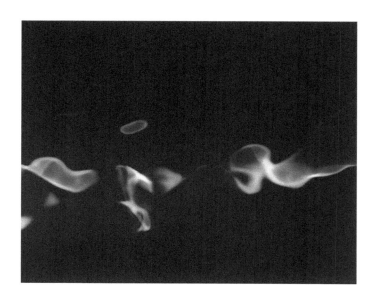

## 33

A month ago there was a distressed hawk flying low, shrieking all day and into the evening. A neighbor told us not to worry, that it was only a juvenile hawk *sorting himself out.* He must be sorted now as there is quiet in the skies with only the occasional familiar calls of the adult red-tails circling slowly over.

When I find myself caught in a living-death-by-a-thousand-administered distractions, I wonder if it might help if I also started circling around—*Not to worry, she's just sorting herself out.*

Now that I am at a point in my life where both the beginning and the end horizons are visible, I do have many things sorted: I do not want to die by distraction or to-do lists; I cherish silence; I don't like it when I am mean. I get it about kindness: *It is a bit embarrassing to have been concerned with the human problem all one's life and find at the end that one has no more to offer by way of advice than, Try to be a little kinder.* I know that kindness is a worthy practice for an individual as well as a nation. I also know that true kindness has teeth.

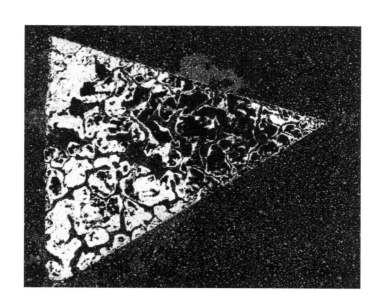

## 34

A friend told me that she was uncomfortable that
I had given away our lesbian secrets in my last
performance piece *My Lunch with Sophia Loren*.
She felt the erotic terrain was too real, too honest.
I responded that I thought there were no lesbian
secrets left, that the cat was out of the bag as it were.
We both agreed that neither of us has seen anything
in mainstream media that would make us say, *Yes!*
*They got that right.*

But this got me thinking about secrets and identity,
etc. You know, sometimes it feels good to get out and
be a lesbian. And sometimes it feels equally good to
stay at home and be a lesbian. The rest of the time I
don't think about it much. I am thoroughly immersed
in my ordinariness—get up, go to work, write, fuss over
the cats, get my teeth cleaned. But today when I met a
new friend, and she showed up in a black leather jacket,
skinny jeans, and black spike heels, well, I was
appreciative.

Maybe lesbian sexuality is more under-known than
secret, which, as another friend points out, lets us stay
under the radar. I think of it like this: a little low flying
keeps me sharp and paying attention.

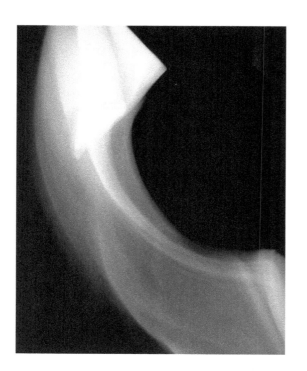

## 35

A master of Kyudo, Zen archery, came to Big Sur
for a demonstration of his art. When ready, he took
his stance. A round target sat in the distance at the
edge of a cliff, at the edge of an ocean, at the edge
of a cerulean blue sky. The crowd stood respectfully.
The archer bowed, kneeled, his gaze inward. Slowly
he rose, attention focused, balance perfect. Years of
training, skill, and devotion showed in the simple beauty
of his stance. Every movement—necessary, effortless.
Every cell awake. He drew the long sinuous bow with
grace and ease. Head, eyes, fist, arrow, focused on the
target to his left. Then, slowly, he turned his head to the
right, away from the target. There was a moment of
tension of his respiratory muscles. Then the release.
The arrow shot out. Up and over the target.
It arced into cloudless sky…boundless ocean.

*Perfect*, the master said.

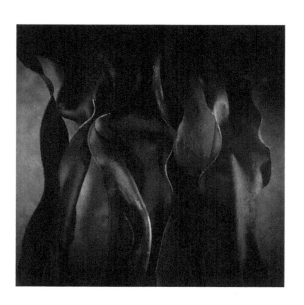

## 36

Early morning beach walk. A light fog. Warm air.
A curious seal makes eye contact. A father teaches
his son to fish. A woman walks her Cairn terrier,
Herbie. Two women pick up trash. A sea otter lies on
its back breakfasting. Two dolphins, cruising side by
side, burst up and out of the water in that arcing flow
that is so gorgeously, breathtakingly *dolphin*.

Later in the evening our boy cat hurtles into the house,
belly down, terror-stricken. My lover goes to see.
She stares into the face of a mountain lion on our deck
a few feet from the front door. Stunned, she forgets to
raise her arms, make noise, and back away slowly.
She is barely able to call out, panic strangling her voice.

Thwarted but undaunted, the mountain lion, who
because of the drought has come close to town for
food, for water, casually turns and walks to the end of
the deck. It jumps up to the hillside and then casually
saunters next door, all grace and muscle and grandeur,
as if nothing in any of this were unusual.

## 37

*To be a writer one must like sentences.*
I hadn't thought of this before, although now
it seems so obvious. I've always loved words
and I am particularly fond of the fragment.
But sentences—of course. They help pull it
all together, don't they?

I have a sentence I've been waiting to use sometime
somewhere. A writer once proposed that any story
will be more interesting if at the end you add, *And
then everything burst into flames.* I keep coming across
this in my notebook and laugh every time I read it,
although I understand well the shadowy undertone.

I am in the high desert of Oregon, writing a story
about Alaska. Some day I'll write about this place,
where at 8:30 last night a long streak of light flamed
blistering gold across the far edge of the playa.
And then everything burst into flames.

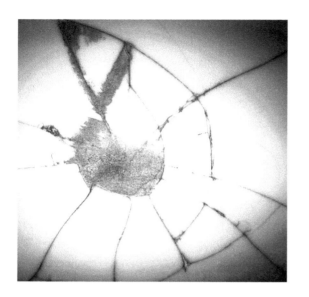

## 38

A rainy day in California.
A fire in the woodstove.
A long-haired girl cat stretched out on my legs.
A friend's essay to read and comment.
And a perfect spiderweb hanging between
two vertical lines of cable that come to the house.
Delicate, drooping threads of silk dotted with droplets
of water strung like silver beads, and not a single tear.

I think that I can't write to you about this because
spiderwebs have been done before, the poets and
authors of children's books and photographers
and painters all in awe. To write about this would be
like painting a sunflower in a field in southern France.

But there it is and I want to share it with you
in all its curvilinear perfection. Its creator is absent
and there is no prey caught in its web for me to say,
*Better luck next time.* It is just this work of art
hanging outside my window, in a gentle rain, with a
wood fire, a cat on my legs, and a story to read about
someone's perfect marriage disintegrating.

## 39

I drove to our monthly women's art group listening
to the news of the massacre in progress in San
Bernardino. *How can I make art of this, yet one
more atrocity?* The painter in our group asked
why I wanted to. *A need.* I replied. *I remember
a performance by Laurie Anderson post 9/11 that was
so elegant, nuanced and soulful, with such integrity,
that I started to breathe again.*

*Here's what I do*, the painter said, *I tell myself, Don't
think. Just paint. And then I make dark miserable
little paintings.* We all laughed. She showed us one
of her paintings which was dark, but not miserable,
and we laughed again, because we all understood the
need for making dark miserable little paintings.

I thought I would come home and pick up oil pastels,
but instead I am writing this, my dark miserable little
ramble. I imagine a large sheet of thick white art paper.
Angled up from bottom left to upper right, strong thick
rust-colored marks; near the center, a slash of red
through a circle of raw white, with thin jaggedy black
lines over-laid; a broad splotch of black high up on the
left, and in it a cluster of tiny dots, midnight blue; the
entire right edge of the paper torn.
　　*Savagery.*
　　That's the word I am looking for.

## 40

My favorite style of journal is out of print a
not been able to find one I like as much. No
too small or too heavy. A paper good for fountain pens,
preferably off-white rather than bright white. A cover
that is supple and feels good to the touch, leather-like,
but not real leather. Rounded corners—very important.
A good color, although basic black will do. Lined or
unlined—I can't decide.

The point after all is to write, not to lose myself in
preciousness. There are so many things to write about:
California is on fire; 700 people crushed to death near
Mecca. Florida is up to no good yet again—it is legal
for lesbians to marry, but not for the non-biological
mother to adopt her own child. *Assholes* is too kind.

Perhaps in lieu of the perfect journal, or assholes or
disasters, I'll write about obsession and perfectionism.
Or perfect ambivalence. Or…oh, this is getting silly.

*What path now?* I ask, *What creative focus?*
I draw the blank Rune—*The Unknowable. Empty-
handed Stepping into the Void.*

To figure out how to live one's life for oneself.
How to get up in the morning.
How to carry on.

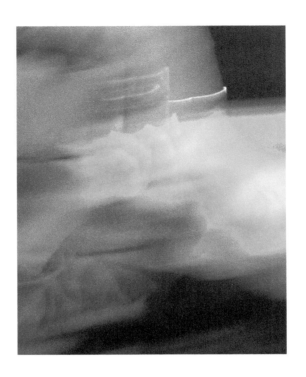

## 41

Mercury went into retrograde yesterday and apparently
will last an entire month, which seems excessive to me.
A week is hard enough. Communications and electronics
will be more problematic than usual—your printer will
jam, your cell phone die, and your boy cat will start
yowling and spraying in the house and hunting the girl cat,
and you'll be angry and think he's a butt until you realize
that something is wrong, and you wish he could speak
English, and it turns out he has a hard-to-treat infection
and now you feel guilty, and you and your partner will
have an awful fight about table manners, and you'll forget
to backup your hard drive, you'll lose a file, and then mis-
place the keys to your office, and if that weren't enough
you realize that you'll be embarrassed if you don't live to
be eighty. Things like that. For a month.

I just thought I'd let you know so you wouldn't be hard
on yourself and you'd take good care and be gentle
with all of life's daily difficulties, because the days
are troubled. The world is on fire.

## 42

Between sky and navy blue is a color called
*Tarantula Blue*. The tarantulas themselves,
*chromatopelma cyaneopubescens*, whose hair
sports this vivid color, cannot see it, which rules
out sexual display as its purpose, or painterly
aesthetics. The color is proliferating in the tarantula
world. And, in terms of optics, the color does not shift
regardless of the angle from which it is observed.
All of this is unusual, even mysterious. Like that ninth
planet that mathematics tells us has to be there, but
has not yet been discovered.

I have never been fond of tarantulas in general,
having encountered several in my desert days,
but this spider, what a beauty—such brazen blue
gorgeousness.

I'm due for more low-lights to my hair—some black
streaks to contrast with the grey. My stylist likes to
drop in one weave of red. It keeps me looking cool,
at least that's what the young man in San Francisco
told me, and the striking young woman at Trader Joe's,
with her hair shooting off in all directions in chunks of
red and black. I think I will ask if this time, instead of
red, we try a weave of *Tarantula Blue*. I like how it
sounds. Vibrant and dangerous.

## 43

My partner's breasts have been altered.
She lost half of one and a chunk of the other
from cancer. They are still beautiful but in a
modern art kind of way. I call them her Picasso
breasts. She likes that. We can both laugh.

There are so many opportunities in life to be humbled:
You can just be wrong; you can clap too early; you can
forget and leave the sunroof of your car open the only
night it rains. You can, like my aunt Evie in a Chinese
restaurant, take a knife and fork to a rolled-up hot hand
towel thinking it is an egg roll. You can sit in stunned
silence when the surgeon clumsily says to your partner,
*If you are done with your breasts, have a mastectomy.*
You can lovingly hold your lover's breasts in your hands
and feel a slip of fear shoot up your arms, slide into your
chest, and coil somewhere near the center of your heart.

# Life Review

In Chinese medicine—*Cold Wet Wind*, with the
overall condition of *Ten Thousand Galloping Horses*.

In astrology—*Taurus, Virgo rising, moon in Libra*.
Seven planets in Aries. Uranus sitting heavy on the
head. *Is life hard?* the astrologer asks.

In the Enneagram—a *4 or a 7*, or both simultaneously.

Some say *anxiety with a depressive overlay*. But I
prefer the word *Melancholia*—the way it slides
down the walls. Chews on the baseboards.

## 44

A small yellow bird drops to the deck, hops to my feet
on the other side of the sliding glass door, and looks up.
I return its gaze. Neither of us moves. A very short time
passes that feels very long. The bird flies away.
I become me again and go about daily life.
But I am not the same. Something has happened.

30,000 years ago someone carved a bird out of ivory.
It's one of the oldest works of art known to us.
Two inches long, a water bird of some kind.
Neck extended, ready to dive under.
A beautiful thing.

Welcome, small yellow beautiful thing
who comes to me this day.
Welcome, breath of the soul.

45

A poet asked the members of the audience if they knew
what a broadside was, because he was talking about his
collaboration with a printmaker, and he was getting
ready to launch into a long anecdote about how
beautiful the final work was, and how they made it, and
their enthusiastic folly of printing about 2500 too many,
and how they ended up just giving them away, but he
stopped himself, realizing that the audience—made up
mostly of local folk, ranchers, and people who love the
remote outback, and who were there this particular
evening because they also liked poetry and art and were
curious to see and hear what the artists and writers were
up to—that this audience might not know what he was
talking about. So he asked: *Does everyone here know
what a broadside is?* The swift response from the
auburn-haired, boot and jeaned, no-nonsense-looking
woman sitting in the chair over by the window was,
*I've got a barn and a rifle. Will that help?*

## 46

No wind, no clouds; early morning walk
on the playa of a saline lake in the outback
of Oregon. I am meeting new birds, delighting
in alkali crusts that puff apart when I toe them.
A bleached-out twig here, stone there, huge
footprints of a sandhill crane, a green marsh,
a clump of past-bloom wild iris, a field of small
yellow flowers.

I am always learning how to live. The long slow
walk in which I rely on my ears, not my eyes.
The sweet call of the meadowlark to my left,
the gurgly trill of the red-winged blackbird in
the tree to my right, the clucking *chef chef chef*
of the northern harrier, the sweet high notes of
a yellow warbler, the silence of the falcon on the
fencepost.

When I arrived here I asked if there were snapping
turtles in the pond. Three days ago I wrote something
difficult about my mother. Then I went to eat, sent an
email, bought something online, talked to a friend, read,
ate some more, watched a movie. I even vacuumed.
I hadn't known what waited below the surface,
its powerful jaws ready to clamp down.

There are so many hungers. Some that cannot be fed.

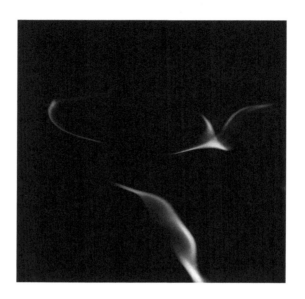

## 47

A blackbird picks up thin stems of straw grass that
have blown onto the deck. When she lands, I turn
and look. This interrupts my writing. She grabs a sprig
and flies up under the eaves. She has chosen the top
of the patio light fixture for her nest. As she goes about
nest building, her mate sits on the deck railing—
guarding, I assume. I return. The female comes close
to the bottom of the sliding glass door of the deck. She
grabs a twig, stops, drops the twig, looks inside. We
have a moment, she and I. Then she picks up the twig,
flies to her nest.

*Give us one more example*, the instructor said, *about
your mother, to help us understand the peril, the cut-off
love. It should be easy. Four sentences is all you need.*
But it is not easy. It is a story that slips away from me
no matter how brave I try to be.

I hope the birds' nest will be strong and safe, that their
chicks will hatch and live, that my presence does not
disturb, cause them to abandon their eggs.
I know so little about blackbirds, only a poem.

## 48

This morning I wonder: *Should I feed the cats now
or later? If I let them out now is it too early?
Will they be snatched up by owls, or coyotes,
or torn up by raccoons?*

On days like this, a letter from a friend, or a phone call,
unbolts my heart. And I just discovered Franz Liszt's
*Consolation #3.*

Last week the US conducted a string of drone strikes
in Yemen, at least forty people killed. Soon the US and
Russia will begin testing militarized dolphins and sea
lions in the Black Sea. Oh, good grief. Where there were
words, now
nothing.

Dadaab, Kenya is the site of the largest refugee center
in the world. A half-million people stranded, without
even enough holes in the ground to shit in.
A man, half-starved, sells his food ration for the week—
a half cup of maize, a teaspoon of sugar—to pay for a
phone call to his wife. His only solace.

What sense—these sufferings?
No sense. No sense at all.

## 49

I have a friend who was born with the happy gene.
He always has a plan. Everything pans out for him.
He's successful in work and love. He's a good friend.
He has never broken a bone, has no diseases, no aches
and pains; his body feels the same as when he was
twenty. He can trigger envy faster than I can spit.

I was not born with the happy gene. I don't plan easily
or well. I improvise. Sometimes it works. I often find
life hard. I am not spiritually evolved. My favorite
literary form is the rant. I am afraid of dying and not
having something witty, wise, or loving to say with my
last breath—*Bye* will probably be it, with a quick
wave of my hand.

But I do have a plan—perhaps my only plan—to
practice an intimacy with all things. Easy to do
with the good stuff, harder with the horrible stuff—
the legs blown off, the cat tortured to death.
During survival training in Alaska they taught us,
*If you accidentally chop off your hand, first thing
you should do is sit down and smoke a cigarette.*
Which was oddly calming.

## 50

On the pond, two coots with two red-headed
chicks in the rushes; a pair of Gadwall ducks
serenely floating. Russian olive trees with dreamy
soft silvery leaves. The lush civility of a large lawn;
the sweeping immensity of the playa; the pale blue-grey
of the shallow lake. A swath of huge Icelandic red
poppies with their purple seed interiors. An overgrown
garden. A row of rhubarb. Everywhere I look—

And later, the ludic—something that causes me to jam
on the breaks and pull over. Twenty or more recently
sheared lambs of different colors, perfectly poised,
unmoving, facing this way and that, on various levels of
hay stacked like Lego blocks by the side of the road.
The absurd smashes into the sublime. I've come full
circle.

## 51

It's true; I've gone over to the other side.
No, not that. I remain chauvinistic to my tribe
even if there has been significant dispersal.
Sometimes I wonder, where did everyone go?
It just changes and then changes some more.

Distant thunder. Hot. Torpid. Hopefully rain.

But what I was starting to say is this:
I have become a birdwatcher. I never thought
this would happen to me—tennis hat, khaki pants,
binoculars, bird book in hand. Yesterday, when the
resident manager asked how I was doing, I chirped
away with the zeal of the newly converted—*A great
morning! I saw a flock of avocets, a grey northern
harrier, two trumpeter swans, and either a whimbrel or
an adolescent long-billed curlew, I am not sure which.*

Hmm; probably too much information.
I think she only wanted to know if I was OK.

Lightning. Rain. A raptor—Vanished.

## 52

I've been doing some skying. Some laking,
some day-dreaming and lollygagging.
Deep in the world of ten thousand things.

I'm not sure the two coot chicks made it. By now
they should be paddling around following mom
and dad. Every day I go to look. The parents carry
on with carrying on.

At the reservoir: Cedra aglow with immersion.
She follows the river downstream. Further than she
intended. Marvels at all the creeks feeding the river,
the ferns, grasses, tendrils floating long—*An entirely
new ecosystem*, she exclaims. Helen swims further and
further to the center where few of us ever go. Laura
swims to the edges, into the rushes—in search of what?
*A redwing blackbird nest with eggs. Their eggs are a
beautiful shade of blue, lighter than robin's eggs, with
splashes of mauve as if flicked by a paintbrush.*

These women—artists—are less than half my age.
Talented, smart, and funny. They still have their knees.
I feel both near and far.
So much at stake.

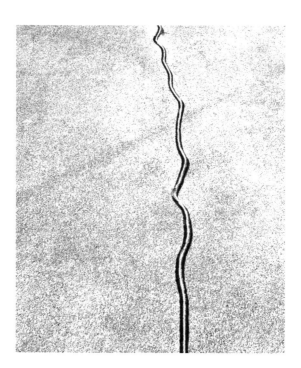

## 53

I knew how this writing was going to end. I had the concluding sentence. But then I immediately forgot it. In Nepal, the Sherpas had a favorite saying—*ke garné*—which translates roughly as, *Oh well*. No matter what happened, if we got lost, or the stove wouldn't light—*ke garné*. I burned my only long-sleeved shirt trying to dry it by the fire. *Ke garné*. The nuance is different from the English; in Nepalese the phrase lacks any hint of cynicism or resignation; instead it feels comforting and reassuring, a beloved uncle sitting beside you, his arm around your shoulders.

I drove up the mountain today without a map. The biker-dude said it was beautiful up there, a good view. The directions were vague and the forest road signs torn down. I drove through the cows and their skittish calves, drove past sage, lupine, up and up until the tall pines and snow. I took a small rutted dirt road off to the right. I was going for the edge, the Big View. I was not unafraid—no one knew where I was, there was no phone service and cars break down etc., etc. Ke garné. I drove until a fallen tree, rocks, and deep ruts stopped me. I might have been able to make it by going around, but I turned back. No big view, no edge. Yet I was happy. Cows, sage, lupine, pines, snow. I had satisfied the day. I still don't remember where I was going when I started this. Or the last line. So I'll just end.

Life Review

Aging is Absurd!

## 54

I only remember the sign, not what the artist
looked like. I think he was young, but I am not sure.
Young and hirsute. I don't remember which war, or
troubles.
He held a sign:

**Bad Things Are Happening.**

I imagine myself now, standing on an empty stage,
not young, but old, or at least, oldish, a face lined
with experience, silver-grey hair, night-blue metal
glasses, dressed simply, but stylishly—
performance black, *naked*
*under my clothes.*
I hold a sign:

**Bad Things Are STILL Happening.**

It is the least I can do, bear witness.

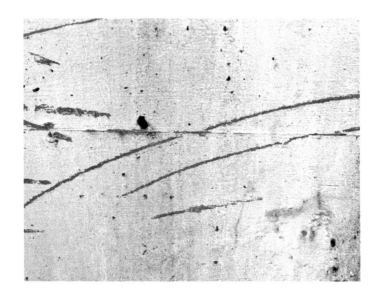

## 55

A morning was rich in birds:
yellow-headed blackbird,
black-crowned night heron,
cinnamon teal duck, red-shafted flicker,
hooded merganser, meadowlark,
caspian tern, avocet in rust and black.
A group of feathery white swans
drifted dreamily with the current. Periodically
they gathered into a small circle and at some unseen
signal simultaneously ducked their heads down,
their fluffy white asses waving gracefully,
absurdly in the air.

It's often a surprise what delights us.
Some things we know well about ourselves:
perhaps you love chocolate, or periwinkle. Pickleball.
I am in love with the big questions:
*Why?* and *Why not?* and
*Have I Loved Well Enough?*

When I moved to California from Canada
it took me a long time to learn to hug.
Once I dreamt I was a refrigerator.
Things are better now.

## 56

One day a friend's favorite cat, Griffy, was acting
inexplicably angry, hostile, and aggressive.
There was no medical reason for his behavior—
he was in perfect health. So my friend consulted
an animal whisperer, who advised, *Pictures, not words,*
*work best when you want to communicate with cats.*
So my friend asked Griffy in pictures, *What's going*
*on?* In true cat perversity, he responded in words, not
pictures (don't ask me how this works), and said,
*You are crazy, lady.*

Dismayed, my friend asked the whisperer if she
herself would check in with Griffy. When she did,
he apologized. He felt bad about his behavior.
He asked the whisperer to tell my friend that he
was sorry. He had been having a bad day.

There's no point to this story except that it delights
me, and it delights me that it delights me.
The election, 2016, has taken its toll.
I thought I had lost my sense of humor.

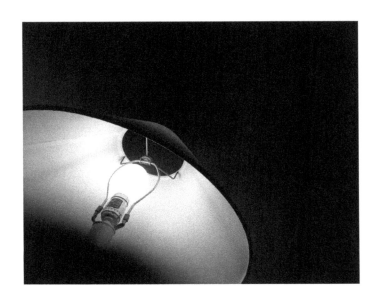

## 57

*Barn's burnt down/now/I can see the moon.*

November, 2016. Awful month. Awful year.
The office next door to mine caught fire.
The sprinkler system and the firefighters
saved my office but in so doing flooded it.
I had to move out. In the same week I developed
severe vertigo doing an exercise for health and
vitality. Then the election.

And even though I knew it was there, in the
madness of my mind I could not see the moon.

But out on the trail I encountered a lovely old
dyke who was friendly and assumed correctly
a camaraderie, a queer intimacy, which warmed
my heart. We talked of needs: to yet again march,
rally, resist. To not turn away.

And the poets are writing; the comedians
are blistering and brave.

What is unleashed shadows the moon.

## 58

I no longer begin my day by reading the news
other than a quick glance to see if we've started
a new war.

On our rural street we fight a developer—his
ugly dense condo project planned for a small
sloping meadow that lies next to a chapel across
from a cemetery and organic farmland. We are a
neighborhood that the city once pledged to protect.

I am learning the hard, tedious, and unglamorous
work of organizing. I am learning also the beauty
of my neighbors—those who have come together
to oppose this ill-conceived project. We work around
our oddities and capabilities. We file another lawsuit.
We have tea, chocolate, and persimmons. Laughter.
Gossip too. Judy's mother fell and broke her hip.
I'm over the flu. Ellen wants the name of my
handyman. Chester down the street is dying.
And last night a mountain lion tore the face off
a neighbor's goat.

Life goes on. I bring the cats in early.

## 59

I just turned seventy. May 2, 2017. The lead-up was
frightening. But now it's back to business as usual,
paddling, head down, leaning into it. Husserl said
there were two ways to face the existential dilemma
of existence: one was to hurl yourself off the cliff
and trust that the ocean would be there to hold and
embrace you. I can't remember what the second was.
I have always felt more at home in the water than land
*Madam Poisson* and all. So off the cliff it is.

My friend/teacher/mentor has Alzheimer's. She is
watching herself lose her mind. *I'm halfway there,
enough to be able to watch the process*, she says.
*Can't turn back so I might as well be interested.*
She tells me she is losing the alphabet. That her
memories, her knowledge, are stored under each
letter, but as she loses the letters she loses her mind.
*Fascinating*, she says. *Yesterday the email: the L
 tetter you sent was so  wondter. Hard to write all,
Love to Canne.alas, the w riter.*

I love this woman. She saved my life as a teenager,
intellectually and emotionally. The finest teacher
I have ever had. I write every two weeks. She enjoys
my letters. When I visit and we hug, she nestles her
head into my neck and rests it there. She wants to
make sure I know she loves me. For a few minutes
I am the ocean.

## 60

When I was a child my father would return
my letters with misspelled words circled in red.
Nonetheless, I remain fond of letter writing.

I used to write long letters to my 8th-grade
summer camp counselor, Linda. She was fun
and kind and very tall. She lived in Illinois
and was a biologist, which I thought was cool.
She was also calm and unafraid in the face of
our adolescent wretchedness. She could confront
without shaming. For this, and for the safe harbor
of her friendship, I remain grateful.

We wrote regularly for a year or two. I entered
high school and felt lost. A brain and a heart
I did not know how to use. A budding lesbian
with forbidden longings. An outsider wanting
in. Only now do I understand how compassionate
she was. I knew so little about compassion then.

I would love to write her a letter again, with my
favorite fountain pen, on stationary I brought back
from Paris. I would tell her I dove deep and found
abundance, found bioluminescent life.

## 61

Is it only here in Santa Cruz where a tech guy would answer my urgent query re: my laptop, mouse, and external keyboard all simultaneously refusing to function by texting that, *Mercury is in retrograde and ends on December 22, so not to worry, it will clear.* And who have I become that it makes perfect sense and I feel relieved? Only one week to go and all will be well. If only this would apply to politics as well as electronics.

On another matter: California is still burning; sharks are freezing to death on the East Coast; and the president snarks that some global warming would be useful right now, har, har. We are in a political bombogenesis, the scientific term for a bomb cyclone, a storm that drops 24 millibars of pressure over 24 hours. It's what got the sharks. It's been a hard year. One vulgarity after another. I have to remind myself to relax my tongue.

Now, January, 2018. Mercury is not in retrograde, my computer works, but Ursula Le Guin has died and it's a quiet grief. She gave me the gift of dragons. I begin to read *No Time to Spare: Thinking About What Matters.* She wastes no time; it's pure Ursula— *The meaning of life is cats, and old age is for anyone who gets there.*

## 62

Last night I asked my dreams for help.
I dreamt a bunch of chickens were stabbing
at a banana peel to get to the fruit inside.

Sometimes dreams can be so mean.

If I lose sight of the shore, if a fire rages
uncontrolled, if I forget that I will never
figure out how to live, what then do I need
to know to live?

Years ago at a local Irish pub, I went to the bar
for a glass of water. There was a rough-edged man,
drunk and a bit crazy, sitting there talking to his
voices. As I stood next to him he turned to me
and growled, *I just don't know, I just don't know.*
With a clarity and compassion that surprised us both,
I looked at him and said, *I just don't know either.*

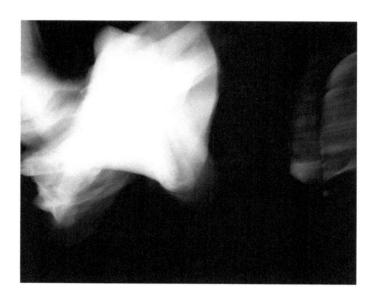

## 63

Some researchers have recently concluded that
between cats and dogs, it's cats that actually
have more brain matter (adjusting for size and weight),
but raccoons are smarter than both cats and dogs.

I think we are all in it together equally. Cats are brilliant
as cats, raccoons as raccoons. I do not embrace my
species as superior. I think we could use a little
refinement, as could knees.

My cats will pounce on any wriggling, moving thing.
I am less prone to indiscriminate pouncing, and I do not
bring home half-dead bats, or their equivalent, to my
lover. I do at times bring home my weariness, my
troubles, my fears about—if I just say the word
*Politics*, will that suffice? If I am lucky and my lover
is having a good day, she will put her arms around me,
her hands warm and gentle on my face.
*Oh sweetheart.*

## 64

Who knows if today is the day when a drone
drops a package at my front door. One I didn't
order, but one Amazon thought I might want.

Who knows if today is the day a drone
strikes, only here, not *there*.
Or a bridge collapses.
Or my heart says *enough*.

Absent for years
today could be the day my sister calls—
Or someone, something, from out
there in the galaxy responds.

If I could save one thing—the lemurs
of Madagascar, Arctic ice—
If I could look up and not be afraid.
If I could have the skies—
uncluttered
unburdened—

I would choose the skies.

## Life Review

Take notes. Lots of notes.
Even though you think you won't,
you will forget.

Naps are good.
So is doing the dishes.

Beware certainty.
Do your best with ambiguity, if only
because it is more interesting.

Hold fire in one hand.
Hold ice in the other.
The heart will understand.

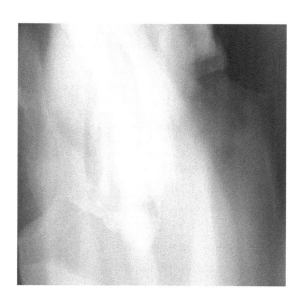

# Postlogue

I miss the cats. The girl slipped out between
my feet one evening and never slipped back in.
A coyote. It's good we didn't find remains.
Three months later we put the boy down. Our
handsome boy—a skeletal wreck from lymphoma.
We wrapped him and buried him deep enough.
We covered his grave with rocks and bricks. And
then a coyote tunneled in and dragged the carcass
away. Left only the shroud.

Years ago, I had an accident that shattered my knee.
It was three long three years and four surgeries to recover.
Something changed in me—from the pain, the drawn-
out effort. Something I felt, but could not quite name:
My teacher said—and I love her for this—
*You've learned how mean life is.*

Now the pandemic. I am healthy. So far.
Sometimes I forget how old I am.
It came as a shock, that because of my age,
I am in a high-risk category. This gets me
special hours for shopping.

I continue to hope that one day life will be easier.
A sweet, wishful thinking. My true wish, though,
toughened up, as I embrace the wind, the coyote,
the shroud, is that the incomprehensible will tell
its own tale.

# Notes

The title, *Difficult Beauty*, was inspired by Steve Haruch's endorsement of the memoir *Crying in H Mart* by Michelle Zaumer: *I'm grateful for its funny, self-deprecating and wise observations, and for its difficult beauty.*

Prologue: The working title of this book was *Little Rambles*. This was before I knew of the work of the 20th century writer Robert Walser, especially his short sketch, *A Little Ramble*.

*Enlightenment is intimacy with all things.* Jane Hirshfield shared this wisdom from the 13th century Zen monk Dogan Zenji in her workshop *Poetry and the Intimacy with All Things*.

12 *why and why and why*, Natasha Trethewey, *Southern Gothic*.

14 The instructor was my first drawing teacher, the thoughtful and inspiring Howard Ikemoto, who taught at Cabrillo College, Aptos, CA.

20 Wislawa Szymborska was a Polish poet, essayist, and translator. She won the Pulitzer Prize for Literature in 1966. She could be wickedly funny.

22 The suggestion of *despondent* versus *crabby* from an email conversation with Camille Dungy on one of those hard and troubled days.

*Failed masculinity*, from a conversation with Val Hartouni.

25 *Pick up a rifle and...* From a conversation with Camille Norton about a frustrating day she had with some dullish, sluggish university students: *I wanted to pick up a rifle and fire it into the ceiling.*

32 I think the writer was Maya Angelou, from an inspiring lecture/performance she gave at UCSC in what seems like forever ago. She quoted poetry for over an hour, all from memory. Astonishing.

33 *It is a bit embarrassing...* From Aldous Huxley, as quoted in *What About the Big Stuff?: Finding Strength and Moving Forward When the Stakes Are High*, (2002) by Richard Carlson

34 *Maybe lesbian sexuality is more under-known than secret...* From a conversation with Carla Freccero.

35 This story was told in class by my first Qigong teacher/ mentor, Teja Bell.

37 *To be a writer...* I have lost my notes regarding who told me this story and who the writing instructor was.

39 The Laurie Anderson performance was *Happiness*.

The painter is Hildy Bernstein, who skillfully weaves her angst into her thoughtful paintings.

40 Runes are small stones, pieces of bone, clay, etc., bearing markings and carvings. They were originally used as divinatory symbols by ancient Scandinavians and Anglo-Saxons.

*To figure out…* For years I have kept a quote by Zora Neal Hurston from her novel, *Their Eyes Were Watching God*, tucked in my heart: *Two things everybody's got tuh do fuh theyselves. They got tuh go tuh God, and they got tuh find out about livin' fuh theyselves.*

41 *The world is on fire…* From a commiserating conversation with Camille Dungy.

47 A thanks to Lynn Stegner for requesting one more example.

48 Anne Carson was thrumming in the background when I was writing this: *What sense it makes for these two mornings to exist side by side in the world where we live, should this be framed as a question, would not be answerable by philosophy or poetry or finance or by the shallows or the deeps of her own mind, she fears.* From *1=1*, *The New Yorker*, Jan 11, 2016.

52 The word *skying* was used by Annie Dillard, quoting Constable in *The Writing Life*, and given that I am a textual kleptomaniac, I snapped it right up.

54 *I stand here naked under my clothes…* Inspired by a poem found on the back cover of the out-of-print edition of *Sappho's Gymnasium* by Olga Broumas and T. Begley: *she comes naked/alone/under her clothes.*

57 *Barn's burnt down…* From the Haiku by Mizuta Masahide.

Stacey D'Erasmo used the term queer intimacy in her review of *Never Anyone But You*, by Rupert Thomson, *NYT Book Review*, Aug. 19, 2018.

Life Review: *Aging is Absurd!* Have I mentioned that I am a textual kleptomaniac? Well, I'm also a verbal kleptomaniac. A friend, and I wish I could remember who, tossed this out as she was leaving my house, probably in response to our complaints about newly acquired aches and pains: *Aging? Oh Aging is Absurd!*

62 The questions in the third stanza were inspired by several sources:

Paule Marshall in *Praisesong for the Widow: Then she tackled the problem of trying to decide how she wanted to live and what was valuable to her. When am I happy and when am I sad and what is the difference? What do I need to know to stay alive? What is true in the world?*

Andre Gide (I can't remember where I found this): *One does not discover new lands without consenting to lose sight of the shore for a very long time.*

Max Ritvo who pondered the figuring out of life in *Letters from Max* by Sarah Ruhl and Max Ritvo.

Postlogue: *Incomprehension.* I had been searching for the right word, one that opened up with compassion and a big meaning. But nothing seemed quite right. Eventually, I found the word I wanted in the poem *Practice* by Jane Hirshfield: *....I count the names of incomprehension: Sanford, Ferguson, Charleston...*

# Acknowledgments

Grateful acknowledgment to the following publications in which these poems and images first appeared:

*The Colorado Review*—Little Rambles 11, 23
*Brevity*—Little Rambles 15, 34, 49, 61
*Brevity*—Photographs—Little Rambles 20, 40, 49, 61
*Kosmos Journal*—Little Rambles 47
*Rappahannock Review*—Little Rambles and photographs 33, 59, 62
*Ruminate*—Little Rambles 46
*Second Wind, Words and Art of Hope and Resilience*, ed. Kate Aver Avraham and Melody Culver—Little Rambles 15, 18, 19, 33. Photographs—*Untitled (pondering in the dunes), Untitled (tree roots on the Big Island), Untitled (Big River, Mendocino), Untitled (water tower, Mendocino), Untitled (Trees UCSD)*.

I would also like to thank the following institutions for the gifts of time, place, good food, and artistic camaraderie that supported the development of the poems and images for this book:

The Djerassi Foundation
Playa Art Residency
Red Cinder Creativity Center
Tyrone Guthrie Center for Art

A very special thanks to my partner Canon Western. Your cancer and my ensuing (temporary) inability to do anything other than make bone broth, go to work, and help care for you, in an odd way led to this project. I thank you for fighting fiercely to stay alive. Thank you for keeping the writing real. Thank you for years of love and care.

There are many people, friends, writers, artists, poets, birdwatchers, and philosophers, who have graced this work in many different ways and I am grateful to you all.

Camille Dungy—you gave me the original idea and inspiration, and then added in your friendship. Thank you mightily.

Karen Zelin—your deep friendship, love, laughter, and ongoing cheerleading of this project has sustained me throughout. *Poof!*

E.G. Crichton—so patient with my endless questions and dithering: thank you for your astute eye, for the three fine-point colored pens I use for editing. And years of collaboration and great food.

Camille Norton—Thank you for embracing this work, and for understanding the importance of the images as well as the text. I love your wit, wisdom, and incisive irreverence.

Lisa Andrews, epistolary friend—as this book took shape, you were generous with thoughtful and detailed suggestions and comments. So helpful.

Kater Pollock—thank you for cracking the whip to keep me on task, and for the first-round of significant editing.

My friend, the late Ellen Greenfield—we both understood the need for the Yiddish phrase, laughing *mit yashtsherkes*— laughing with tears in your eyes. I miss you terribly.

Marilyn DuHamel—thank you for the tea and cashews, your gentle ways, and for staying connected all the way through.

Lynne Stegner—you named and defended what I was up to early on; basically, that little things go vast. And goofy can be a part of it all.

Annetta Kapon—you once said to me on one of those self-doubting days, *Cut the shit, Lauren*. A perfect moment; I am still laughing.

Martha Casanave, photographer extraordinaire—thank you for your perceptive comments, commiseration, and years of cartoons and laughter.

Madeline Spencer—birdwatching mentor, late-in-life friend (such a gift), and *grammar consultant par excellence*, thank you for it all.

Jennifer Sweeney—you were brave with the deletes and the rearrangements, and you saw what I could not see.

Victoria May—Art Director of the Universe, I wrap my arms around your wit, skill, and perspicacity.

Although I wrote the first *Little Rambles* (the title I used originally) without knowing his work, I want to acknowledge the 20th century writer, Robert Walser, especially his short essay *A Little Ramble*.

And finally, many thanks to my publisher Kate Hitt of Many Names Press. Your passion for poetry and image is a joy. Thank you for bringing *Difficult Beauty* into the world.

To all my readers—my gratitude and heartfelt thanks.

# About the Author

Lauren Crux is an artist whose work oscillates between performance, photography and writing. She obtained an MFA in interdisciplinary studio arts from UC Irvine. She has written and performed five full-length performance monologues: *Dinosaurs & Haircuts*: *On Blind Dates and Unexpected Encounters*; *My Lunch with Sophia Loren and Other Stories*; *Starting from the Wrong Place*; *OUTTAKES: Monologues, Stories, and Social Commentary*; *On Being Cool and Other Digressions*; and *Two Truths and A Lie*. She has also co-created and performed in several collaborative community-based art projects. Her poetry, prose and photography have been published in a variety of journals and anthologies—recently, *Kosmos*, *Rappahannock Review*, *Ruminate*, *Brevity*, *The Colorado Review*, *Memoir Magazine*, *phren-z*, and *TRIVIA*.

Her honors include the James Irvine Foundation Honorary Fellowship, a major project grant from the Arts Research Institute of UCSC, as well as fellowships at the Djerassi Resident Artist Program, the Virginia Center for the Creative Arts and the Tyrone Guthrie Centre, Ireland. In 2016 she was awarded the LGBTQ Lifetime Achievement Award of Santa Cruz County, California. She is a psychotherapist and lives in Santa Cruz, California.

www.laurencrux.com

# Colophon

Award-winning letterpress printer, book artist and poet Kate Hitt established Many Names Press in 1993 for literary writers and fine artists to broadcast their exemplary works through creative collaboration with a like-minded small press publishing house.

Among the esteemed poets, writers and artists Many Names Press has produced over the years are: fine artists Douglas McClellan, William S. Stipe (Uncle Bill) and Andrea Rich; poets Jerry Martien, Louise Grassi Whitney, Hermie Medley, Maude Meehan, Clair Killen, Margarite Tuchardt, Amber Coverdale Sumrall and Patrice Vecchione; writers and poets Becky Taylor and Dena Taylor; and novelist Leba Wine.

Kate is a founding member of the Kunsang Gar Center with her friend and mentor Geshe Dangsong Namgyal, a Tibetan lama. She is a member of the Santa Cruz Printers Chappel, a past board member of the Diversity Center in Santa Cruz, and the president of the Friends of the Arcata Library. She holds an English degree in Comparative Literature from the University of Virginia, has studied digital design at Cabrillo College, fine hand bookbinding with Constance Hunter, and is a graduate of Leadership Santa Cruz.

After 30-years plus in Corralitos and Santa Cruz, California, Kate has returned to Humboldt County.